QUIMBANDA MAGIC SPELLS

THE SECRETS OF AFRO-BRAZILIAN SPIRITUALISM

THE SECOND EXU KINGDOM OF THE CROSSINGS

CARLOS ANTONIO DE BOURBON-GALDIANO-MONTENEGRO

AMERICAN CANDOMBLE CHURCH PUBLICATIONS, LOS ANGELES

QUIMBANDA MAGIC SPELLS

THE SECRETS OF AFRO-BRAZILIAN SPIRITUALISM

THE SECOND EXU KINGDOM OF THE CROSSINGS

AMERICAN CANDOMBLE CHURCH PUBLICATIONS

P.O. BOX 881377

LOS ANGELES, CALIFORNIA 90009

LEGAL DISCLAIMER

No part of this book may be reproduced in any manner without written permission from the publisher or the author of this book. This book contains formulas that were used in the historical AFRO-BRAZILIAN religious practices of Quimbanda, Candomble, Macumba and Umbanda. The author and the publisher do not encourage any of the practices in this book nor do we assume any liabilities for presenting those formulas or any information in this book. The formulas are presented for curious only. Neither the author, *Carlos Antonio De Bourbon-Galdiano-Montenegro* nor the publisher, *American Candomble Church* assumes any responsibilities for the outcome of any of the spells, rituals or initiations in this book. We make no claims to any supernatural powers of these traditional initiation rituals. All inquiries or comments may be directed to the publisher. You must be at least 18 years of age or older to purchase this book or to purchase any of the supplies listed herein.

TABLE OF CONTENTS

BOOK DESCRIPTION

This book contains information about the sacred spells and rituals of the Afro-Brazilian religious tradition of Quimbanda. This particular book contains information about how to do spells and powerful rituals for the Spirit, **Exu Rei Dos Sete Cruzeiros** and the Spirit, **Pomba Gira Reina Dos Sete Cruzeiros** of the ***Second Lesser Quimbanda Kingdom*** also known as *The Kingdom of the Seven Crossings* (*REINO DOS SETE CRUZEIROS*).This book also contains information about how to do spells and rituals for the nine (9) Chief Guardian Exus that govern over the Quimbanda Kingdom of the Crossings.

AN INTRODUCTION TO BRAZILIAN QUIMBANDA

The historical roots of the present day Quimbanda religious tradition are distinctly African. The great African slave trade that lasted from 1514 - 1866 brought a lasting African cultural presence to Brazil and to the Americas. *Quimbanda is an Afro-Brazilian religion* practiced primarily in the urban city centers of Brazil. Quimbanda practices are typically associated with prayers and rituals associated with a mixture of various forms of spirituality. Before and even after the African diaspora, the present day religious faith of Quimbanda merged with other religious traditions and it is a mixture of ancient *European Necromancy* and *Sorcery, Congo religious traditions, indigenous native Indian beliefs from the Amazon Rain Forest, European Spiritualism* and the *Jewish Kabbalistic magical religious tradition*.

Over the course of 500 years of shaping in the New World, the Quimbanda faith, through spiritual evolution has emerged and become a very distinct religious belief that is widely accepted as a legitimate religious tradition.Although distinctly different from its original religious practice which had its roots in the African Congo, the religious concept is identical in terms of religious structure and ritual practice.

The word Quimbanda (Kimbanda) actually comes from the African Bantu word meaning “healer” or “shaman.” Quimbanda also refers to *"the one who communicates with the beyond"*.

“The Quimbanda magico-religious tradition is the most powerful Congo magical practice found in the New World and is also known and revered as perhaps being the most dynamic, complicated and the most powerful forms of African magico-religious practices found in Latin America”. Quimbanda was originally contained under the Afro-Brazilian religious tradition of Macumba. In the Mid-20th Century, Macumba split into two religions: Quimbanda and Umbanda. Umbanda represented the more popular with many Christian elements of Macumba, while Quimbanda retained the distinctively African traits. Quimbanda has continued to distinguish itself as a religion, while resisting many, but not all of the Catholic and French Spiritism influences that have penetrated Umbanda and other Afro-Brazilian religions.

The Quimbanda religion was first brought to the United States in the 1920's by the *De Bourbon-Montenegro Family* who have a long history and involvement with traditional Afro-Brazilian religions since the year 1864. The Quimbanda religion has been increasing in popularity in recent years with new converts and practitioners from all around the world and from every socio-economic and ethnic walk of life. The reason for its rise in popularity is that the religious philosophy and spiritual practice of the Quimbanda religion answers questions to the meaning of life and it also quickly resolves through spirituality the problems associated with our everyday life. The rituals of Quimbanda spiritualism gives individuals a sense of control over their lives through spiritual self-empowerment to believe in themselves and their spiritual birth destiny.

Religious practitioners of the Quimbanda religion become aware of the great power and mysteries found within nature and their spiritual surroundings. *Through a series of progressive initiation rites associated with the Quimbanda religious faith, individuals become responsible individuals and have a greater respect for the environment and the Universal Mysteries of God.*

In the year 2003, *Carlos Antonio De Bourbon-Galdiano-Montenegro* founded the first legal church of Afro-Brazilian religious traditions in the United States, the *American Candomble Church*. The *American Candomble Church* was founded to establish a religious community and cultural center for the practice of the Afro-Brazilian religious faiths of Candomble De Congo and Quimbanda.

The Quimbanda religious tradition and its powerful spiritual philosophy are no longer confined to Brazil and religious practitioners can be found in just about every country of the World.

THE QUIMBANDA RELIGIOUS PHILOSOPHY

The Quimbanda religious tradition is monotheistic. Monotheism is the belief in the existence of one Supreme God. Religious initiates of the Quimbanda religion refer to him as ***Nzambi*** or ***Nzambi Mpungu***, *"Almighty God of the Great Celestial Mysteries and the Creator of the Heavens and the Earth"*. In the Quimbanda religious tradition, God is also referred to as ***Nzambi Ntoto***. In the religious context of our theology, the word Nzambi Ntoto means "God Who touched and walked the Earth". The religious initiates of Quimbanda also refer to God as ***Ndala Karitanga*** (*God who created Himself*) and *Sa Kalunga* (*Lord Endless, Infinite and Supreme God*), after having created the world and everything in it. Although many religious practitioners of Quimbanda would consider its religious philosophy as monotheistic, there are many elements of pantheism which have been incorporated within the confines of the belief of one true God.

Pantheism is the view that the Universe (Nature) and God are identical and that the essence of God is found within the Cosmos as an all-encompassing unity and the sacredness of Nature.

There has been in recent years much debate and confusion about the Quimbanda religion as being polytheistic, but it is not. It is difficult to delineate from notions such as pantheism and monotheism. The confusion comes from the lack of understanding between the concepts of the term “worship” and the term “veneration.”

Worship is an act of religious devotion usually directed to one or more deities.

Veneration is a special act of honoring a saint: a dead person who has been identified as singular in the traditions of the religion.

In the world of Quimbanda, we worship God and venerate the deities or spirits (*Nkisi*). Catholics venerate the saints, (among them Mary), as human beings who had remarkable qualities, lived their faith in God to the extreme and are believed to be capable of interceding in the process of salvation for others; however, Catholics do not worship them as gods.

There are other examples of monotheistic religions such as Christianity which embrace the concepts of a plurality of the divine; for example, the Trinity, in which God is one being in three eternal persons (the Father, the Son and the Holy Spirit). Additionally, most Christian churches teach Jesus to be two natures (divine and human), each possessing the full attributes of that nature, without mixture or intermingling of those attributes.

Although there can be found in the African continent as well as many other places of the world the belief in polytheistic religious beliefs and practices, the concept of monotheism in the ancient African continent has existed for over 8500 years and its concept is not new. *The practice of monotheism in Africa predates the birth of Christianity.*

Most of the fear and misunderstanding about the Quimbanda and Candomble religious traditions come from individuals who have a lack of understanding about the religious philosophy of African cultures and their sacred traditions.

Although we often define those spiritual entities venerated and associated with the Quimbanda religious tradition as deities, they are not. The word deity for those practicing traditional Quimbanda at the *American Candomble Church* simply means and refers to an elevated spirit which can be petitioned to intercede on our behalf directly to God and assist us in the process of the spiritual elevation and the evolution of our soul. This concept is the same as the veneration of the Saints by Roman Catholics.

There is only one true God in the Quimbanda religious philosophy and we call him Nzambi, the "*Father and Creator of the Heavens and the Earth*", the "*Creator of all that is "Seen" and "Unseen"*".

THE DEITIES AND THE SPIRITS OF THE QUIMBANDA PANTHEON

If you are going to have success in using the spiritual principles of this book as well as many of my other books written about *Quimbanda* and *Candomble De Congo* religious traditions, it is important for you to understand the religious concept and spiritual function of the deities and the spirits of the powerful *Quimbanda* pantheon. By understanding the spiritual concept of the *Quimbanda* magico-religious system you will be able see very fast and spectacular results in your spiritual requests.

Although there are various forms of traditional Brazilian *Quimbanda* practiced throughout Brazil and the world, and each with its own religious views about how the religion should be practiced and how the *Quimbanda* deities and spirits should be organized, I will present to you in this book the magico-religious system and religious philosophy as practiced by the members of the *American Candomble Church*.

It has been estimated that there are over 65,000 *Quimbanda* religious temples in present day Brazil. *Quimbanda* temples are called *Terreiro* (backyard) or *Tenda* (tent). In Brazil each of the *Quimbanda* temples are autonomous religious organizations that focus around a central spiritual leader.

The spiritual leader of the traditional *Quimbanda* temple is called *"Tata Nganga"* or *"Pai De Santo"*. Both words meaning *"Father of the Mysteries of the Spirits"*.

The *American Candomble Church* is the first and only known legal religious organization in the United States that exists in the world that has been formally organized and structured with members from all around the world and from every walk of life.

This book will only explore the spiritual mysteries of The Seven Lesser Quimbanda Kingdoms of the deity more commonly known as Exu.

The *Quimbanda* religious philosophy believes that the Universe and Earth are divided into Seven Kingdoms or spiritual realms. Each of these spiritual realms has been appointed with spiritual guardians by *Nzambi*. These deities were placed there by *Nzambi* to govern over these realms where these spirits reside.

Each of the Seven *Quimbanda* kingdoms deals with various aspects of how mankind relates to the spirits as found in nature.

The *Quimbanda* concept is very complex, but I will try to explain it in a simple comprehendible manner for the purpose of this book the spiritual principles and sacred theology of the *Quimbanda* religious tradition of the *American Candomble Church*.

The *Quimbanda* pantheon of deities and spirits is composed of seven (7) outer *Quimbanda Kingdoms* and seven (7) inner *Quimbanda Kingdoms*. These sacred kingdoms are known as, *The Greater Quimbanda Kingdoms and The Lesser Kingdoms.*

The realm of Heaven where *Nzambi* resides is not considered a category of one of the *Quimbanda Kingdoms* because he is the "Creator" and it is only through his "Divine Grace" that all of the outer and inner kingdoms exist.

In the *Quimbanda* religious system*, Nzambi* is considered masculine but can create duality in his work and in his sacred creations.

The first three (3) Kingdoms of the *Quimbanda* deities are more commonly known as the *Quimbanda Trinity*. The *Quimbanda Trinity* is composed of the three deities, *Exu Maioral*, *Exu Rei* and *Maria Padilla Reina*. Together these three powerful spiritual forces govern the great cosmos and the universal laws of the Earth for *Nzambi*. That is why the religious practitioners of the *Quimbanda* religion venerate these three deities. The veneration of the *Quimbanda Trinity* is a central spiritual belief of our faith. Religious practitioners of *Quimbanda* believe that the deities of the *Quimbanda* pantheon were placed there by *Nzambi* to watch over the Universe and over the actions of mankind.

Within the realm of the outer confines of the Kingdoms of the *Quimbanda Trinity* there are found the mysteries of the inner *The Seven Greater Quimbanda Kingdoms* and *The Seven Lesser Quimbanda Kingdoms.*

The *Seven Lesser Quimbanda Kingdoms* are governed by and ruled over by the *Quimbanda* deities of King, *Exu Rei* and the Queen, *Maria Padilla Reina*. The deity Queen, *Maria Padilla Reina* is also known as *Pomba Gira* by the religious practitioners of the Quimbanda religious faith.

The deities King, *Exu Rei* and the Queen, *Maria Padilla Reina* are believed to have seven different spiritual paths which are split among *The Seven Lesser Quimbanda Kingdoms*.

Each of *The Seven Lesser Quimbanda Kingdoms* is governed over by a distinct spiritual path of the deities, King *Exu Rei* and the Queen, *Maria Padilla Reina*.

Within each of *The Seven Lesser Quimbanda Kingdoms*, there are 9 Chief Guardian Spirits of *Exu* and *Pombagiras*. These Chief Guardian Spirits of *Exu* and *Pombagiras* are there to assist the king and the queen of each one of *The Seven Lesser Quimbanda Kingdoms*. Each one of these Chief Guardian Spirits of *Exu* and *Pombagiras* are associated with a specific spiritual task and assignment to spiritually assist mankind.

These *Exu* and *Pombagira* spirits operate under the direct command of the King (EXU) and Queen (REINA) that govern a particular *Quimbanda* Kingdom.

Although there are many different individual *Exus* and *Pombagira* spirits represented within the confines of the *The Seven Lesser Quimbanda Kingdoms*, it is believed that there exist 121 different distinct *Exus* and

121 different distinct *Pombagiras* also found within the confines of *The Seven Lesser Quimbanda Kingdoms*. This belief is not shared by all traditional *Quimbanda* temples, but this is the religious philosophy of the *American Candomble Church*.

In the following explanation of *The Seven Greater Quimbanda Kingdoms* and *The Seven Lesser Quimbanda Kingdoms*, the word deity refers to a highly evolved spiritual force that Nzambi placed in charge of a particular *Quimbanda* Kingdom and the word spirit (Nkisi) refers to a spiritual force that is submissive to the deity spirits. In both cases, both forces dominate and have a powerful control and influence over the destiny of human beings.

Although the *Quimbanda* religious tradition believes that these spiritual entities have a great impact and influence on the lives and destiny of all human beings, we also believe that Nzambi at the moment of the "*Divine Act of Creation*" gave human beings the ultimate divine gift which is "freedom of choice" and the freedom to decide what path we should take in this life. This important concept is one of the Seven Principles of the Quimbanda Universal Cosmic Laws.

In the *Quimbanda* religious tradition there is no "right" and there is no "wrong." There are only consequences that result because of our choices and from our decisions.

The *Quimbanda* spirits and deities were placed here by *Nzambi* to assist mankind with whatever decisions that we may chose and to spiritually assist us in manifesting our desires. That is why the *Quimbanda* religious tradition is centered on the veneration of the spiritual deity known as Exu. Exu is the Divine Messenger of the Crossroads of life. When we decide to make a decision, Exu is always there present reminding us that there will be consequences to our actions because we have "freedom of choice". The crossroads of life represent the many consequences or paths that may come our way because of our choices and because we have “freedom of choice”. The religious practitioners of the *Quimbanda* religious tradition believe that the spiritual concept of “freedom of choice” is a “Divine Privilege” bestowed upon mankind by *Nzambi*. “Freedom of choice” is not a right; it is a gift from God.

THE FIRST GREATER QUIMBANDA KINGDOM

Ruled over by the deity, ***EXU MAIORAL*** - Governs the Astral World, the Archangel Metatron, the Seven Archangels (Archangel Michael, Archangel Raphael, Archangel Gabriel, Archangel Uriel, Archangel Anael, Archangel Zerachiel, and Archangel Raziel) & the Astral Spirits of the Cosmos.

THE 72 ASTRAL SPIRITS OF EXU:

Exu Bael, Exu Agares, Exu Vassago, Exu Samigina, Exu Marbas, Exu Valefor, Exu Amon, Exu Barbatos, Exu Paimon, Exu Buer, Exu Gusion, Exu Sitri, Exu Beleth, Exu Leraje, Exu Eligos, Exu Zepar, Exu Botis, Exu Bathin, Exu Sallos, Exu Purson, Exu Marax, Exu Ipos, Exu Aim, Exu Naberius, Exu Glasya-Labolas, Exu Bune, Exu Ronove, Exu Berith, Exu Astaroth, Exu Forneus, Exu Foras, Exu Asmoday, Exu Gaap, Exu Furfur, Exu Marchosias, Exu Stolas, Exu Phenex, Exu Halphas, Exu Malphas, Exu Raum, Exu Focalor, Exu Vepar, Exu Sabnock, Exu Shax, Exu Vine, Exu Bifrons, Exu Uvall, Exu Haagenti, Exu Crocell, Exu Furcas, Exu Balam, Exu Alloces, Exu Camio, Exu Murmur, Exu Orobas, Exu Gremory, Exu Ose, Exu Amy, Exu Oriax, Exu Vapula, Exu Zagan, Exu Volac, Exu Andras, Exu Haures, Exu Andrealphus, Exu Cimejes, Exu Amdusias, Exu Belial, Exu Decarabia, Exu Seere, Exu Dantalion, Exu Andromalius

THE SECOND GREATER QUIMBANDA KINGDOM

Ruled over by the deity, ***EXU REI*** - Governs the Earth & the Underworld with Maria Padilla Reina. Exu manifests and encompasses male sexuality, fertility and strength. ***EXU REI*** is the deity of the Crossroads and the Emperor of the Constellations.

THE THIRD GREATER QUIMBANDA KINGDOM

Ruled over by the deity, ***MARIA PADILLA REINA*** (POMBA GIRA) - Governs over human emotions and desires with Exu Rei. Pomba Gira is viewed as the consort of Exu Rei. Pomba Gira represents female beauty, sexuality, and desire. Pomba Gira is viewed as a beautiful woman who is insatiable. She is venerated with great respect and care, as her worshippers concede that her wrath can be firm and strong. Pomba Gira is often invoked by those who seek aid in matters of the heart and love. The deity of the Crossroads,T-Roads and Empress of the Seven Planets. Within the Third Greater Quimbanda Kingdom there are also many paths of the female spirit known as Pomba Gira which can also manifest within the realms of the Seven Lesser Quimbanda Kingdoms.

THE FOURTH GREATER QUIMBANDA KINGDOM

Ruled over by the ***AJE SPIRITS*** - The four (4) Elements (Air, Fire, Earth, Water) & the fifth (5) Element of Void (Spirit). The Fourth Greater Quimbanda Kingdom is also ruled over by *Iyami Oxorongá*, a powerful witch and the Aje Spirits. The Aje spirits are the daughters of *Iyami Oxorongá*. The Aje Spirits are invisible spiritual entities that coexist with humans here on Earth. It is believed that the Aje Spirits are powerful "witches" that control all aspects of human destiny including such things as happiness, wealth, love, health and personal relationships. It is also believed that if an individual does not make a spiritual peace and truce with the powerful Aje Spirits that they can cause great harm and bring about great tragedy to all human beings. The Aje Spirits were here before the first man and first woman appeared on this Earth. Since the time that man and woman first appeared here on Earth, the Aje Spirits have been in spiritual competition with humans and historically have many of times tried to eliminate all life of mankind through such negative acts as causing famines, disease and even natural catastrophes and disasters such as floods, tornadoes and earthquakes.

THE FIFTH GREATER QUIMBANDA KINGDOM

Ruled over by the ***EGGUN SPIRITS*** - (Ancestors) & Spirit Guides (Preto Velhos)

The Eggun Spirits are our blood related ancestors. Practitioners of the Quimbanda religious tradition venerate the ancestors. The veneration of these ancestor spirits is not a religion in and of itself, but a facet of Quimbanda religious expression which recognizes an element beyond human control. This form of veneration is at the core of all of the religious practices in Afro-Brazilian spiritualism. The basis of ancestor verneration seems to stem from two principle spiritual ideas: (1) that "those who have gone before" have a continual and beneficent interest in the affairs of the living; and (2) more widespread, uneasiness, fear of the dead, with practices to placate them. The Eggun Spirits are a part of the Quimbanda pantheon of divinities. In the African Congo they are referred to as the Egungun. The Egungun represents the "collective spirit" of the ancestors. Through veneration of the ancestors, they assure a place for the dead among the living. It is their responsibility to compel the living to uphold the ethical standards of past generations.

The spirits of the“Preto Velhos” (Old Black Ones) are spirits that represent the elders of the first African slaves to work on the sugarcane and coffee plantations of Brazil. These spirits are believed to assist the followers of the Quimbanda religious tradition with such things as spiritual protection and healing. These powerful entities are also venerated as powerful spirit guides for practitioners from various religious traditions of Afro-Brazilian Spiritualism.

THE SIXTH GREATER QUIMBANDA KINGDOM

Ruled over by the ***CONGO SPIRITS*** (NKISI) - Govern the Physical World of Mankind & Spiritual World of the Dead. It must also be noted here that the nkisi spirits of the Afro-Caribbean Congo religious practices of *Palo Mayombe*, *Palo Monte* and *Kimbisa* would be found within the sixth Quimbanda Kingdom. This information is important to know as there are many initiates from these Afro-Caribbean religious traditions that are currently being initiated into the mysteries of Afro-Brazilian Quimbanda. These spirits as found in the Caribbean would be; ***Kobayende*** - King of the dead, god of diseases. ***Centella Ndoki*** - Gatekeeper between life and death. ***Gurunfinda*** - God of forest and herbs. ***Nkuyu*** - Deity of woods and roads, guidance and balance. ***Madre de Agua*** - Goddess of water and fertility. ***Mama Sholan Guengue*** - Goddess of richness and pleasures. ***Tiempo Viejo***- God of divination and winds. ***Cabo Rondo*** - God of hunt and war. ***Siete Rayos*** - God of thunder and fire. ***Tiembla Tierra*** - Spirit of wisdom and justice. ***Zarabanda*** - Deity of work and strength. The American Candomble Church also houses the spiritual mysteries of the Afro-Caribbean religious tradition of Palo Mayombe. Members of the American Candomble Church are given the opportunity to also initiate into the Afro-Caribbean Congo mysteries as part of their religious educational experience and are able to receive the Nkisi spirit mysteries (Traditional Palo Mayombe Ngangas) of Palo Mayombe. Although the two religious beliefs are distinctly different, they both share the same Congo regional and historical roots. It should also be noted that each of the Nkisi spirits has been assigned with a specific spiritual path of the spirit Exu (Lucero). The Exu spirits (Luceros) found within both religious traditions are submissive to the Nkisi spirits which govern the Sixth Greater Quimbanda Kingdom. *It should also be noted that the religious practitioners of Quimbanda only* ***venerate*** *the Nkisi spirits while many times the religious practitioners of Afro-Caribbean derived Congo religious traditions such as Palo Mayombe, Palo Monte and Kimbisa*

***worship** the Nkisi spirits as gods. This is just one example of the difference between the two Congo derived religious beliefs.*

These are the primary Nkisis recognized at the American Candomble Church in the religious line of Quimbanda Congo spirits;

Aluvaiá - Intermediary between humans and the other nkisis

Nkosi Mukumbe (Roxi Mukumbe) - Nkisi of war and roads.

Mutalambô (Kabila, Lambaranguange) - Hunter, lives in forests and mountains; deity of plentiful food.

Gongobira - Young hunter and fisherman.

Katendê - Knows the secrets of medicinal herbs.

Zaze (Loango) - Delivers justice to humans.

Kaviungo (Kavungo, Kafungê, Kingongo) - God of health and death.

Angorô (male form) and Angoroméa (female) - Assist the communication between humans and deities.

Kitembo (Tempo) - Deity of weather and seasons.

Matamba (Bamburussenda, Nunvurucemavula): Female warrior, commands the dead.

Kisimbi (Samba) -The great mother, deity of fertility, of lakes and rivers.

Kaitumbá (Mikaiá, Kokueto) - Goddess of the sea.

Karunga Njambi - Lives at the bottom of the ocean.

Zumbarandá - The eldest of the gods, connected to death.

Wunje - The youngest of the Nkisis, represents the happiness of youth.

Lembá Dilê (Lembarenganga, Jakatamba, Kassuté Lembá, Gangaiobanda) - Connected to the creation of the world.

The mysteries of the Orixas from the Candomble De Congo (Candomble De Angola) religious tradition are also found within the confines of the Sixth Quimbanda Kingdom. In the Candomble De Congo religious tradition, the Orixas are also considered Nkisi spirits. This is the primary difference between the Santeria religion and the Candomble De Congo religious tradition.

THE SEVENTH GREATER QUIMBANDA KINGDOM

Ruled over by the CABOCLOS - The Guardians of the Earth that governs over the actions of mankind.

The spirits of the "Caboclos" (Indian) are spirits that represent the native Indigenous peoples that the first African slaves encountered when they arrived in Brazil. These spirits are believed to assist the followers of the Quimbanda religious tradition with such things as spiritual protection and healing. These powerful entities are also venerated as powerful spirit guides for practitioners from various religious traditions of Afro-Brazilian Spiritualism. The ***American Candomble Church*** has expanded this religious regional meaning and now includes the spirits of Native Americans from North America.

INTRODUCTION TO SPELL CASTING

The best part about casting Brazilian Quimbanda magical spells and rituals is that they work very fast. All of the following Brazilian Quimbanda spells and rituals are real and authentic. I have personally used all of them over the past years in my spiritual practice of traditional Brazilian Quimbanda with much success. All of the following spells and rituals should be followed exactly as they are presented here in this book if you want to see fast magical results and success.

In order for you to realize the full maximum magical results of working within the Seven Lesser Quimbanda Kingdoms of Exu it is important that you familiarize yourself with each of the Kings and Queens which goven that realm and to know each and everyone of the nine Chief Exu Spirits which reside within that magical kingdom.

There are ten (10) spiritual concepts which you should follow and keep in mind when working with any of the spirits from the Seven Lesser Quimbanda Kingdoms of Exu Rei and Maria Padilla Reina Pomba Gira.

If you follow these ten (10) spiritual concepts as I present them to you in order you will see the successful ritual and magical results that you desire. Remember that part of performing and casting magical spells requires that the individual doing so must approach the spirits with a stable, clean and clear mind and be focused on the desired outcome. The following spiritual formula can be used to invoke and summon each of the spirits from the Lesser Quimbanda Kingdom of Exu and Pomba Gira depending on what your magical desire is. Before beginning any type of spiritual work, it is important to get to know the characteristics and traits for each of the Exus and the Pomba Giras from each of the Seven Lesser Quimbanda Kingdoms.

AN INTRODUCTION TO BRAZILIAN QUIMBANDA RITUALS

The magical spiritual offerings and sacred rituals of the Brazilian Quimbanda religious tradition are known for their fast results. Spiritual offerings and rituals are collectively known in the Portuguese language as "***trabalhos***" or in the English language as "***works***". Spiritual offerings are also known in the African language as "***Ebo***". Because of the historical richness of the Quimbanda religion, the religious practitioners of this magico-religious system draw on the energy found in nature as well as from the powers of the spirits and the deities of the Quimbanda pantheon. Rituals of Quimbanda are usually dedicated to one or more spirits. The rituals usually consist of drawing a symbolic spirit signature on the ground at a sacred location where the ritual offering will be left at. The location of the ritual offering will be determined by what type of Ebo is being cast and for what spirit is being invoked. It is believed that every location has a specific set of spiritual entities that govern that place. A typical Quimbanda ebo would be done at the crossroads when summoning the spirit ***Exu Tranca Ruas*** to close the roads of your enemies. The ebo usually consists of candles, cigars, cigarettes, a food offering, a liquor offering and other items that are sacred to the spirit that is being invoked to do the spiritual work. The majority of the ebo's of Quimbanda are performed during the late night hours because it is believed that the spirits manifest here on earth during those hours. After the ebo has been brought to the desired magical location, the religious practitioner will recite a prayer to the spirits making a spiritual petition to grant their requests. Rituals such as those for cleansing are usually also done at specific locations depending on the desired intent of the individual. Cleansing rituals usually involve the individual taking a series of herbal spiritual baths known as "***amaci***" and often times a ritual performed at the shrine of a particular spirit or deity at the Quimbanda Terreiro, Tenda or Munanzo. The word, ***Terreiro*** in the Portuguese language refers to a traditional Afro-Brazilian temple and the word, ***Munanzo*** is an African Congo word that refers to a house of worship.The priest or religious practitioner who performs these ebo's and rituals is called “Quimbandeiro”. The word Quimbandeiro is an African Congo word meaning “healer” or “shaman”.Because the Quimbanda religion believes in spiritual communication, often times an individual seeking spiritual advice will visit a Quimbandeiro to find out the answer of their questions. This is usually performed using a divination system known as "***Buzios***". The buzios are an Afro-Brazilian divination system which uses a set of 16 cowrie shells to consult with the Quimbanda spirits. This divination method is also known as the “***chamalongo***”. An individual may also seek advice from a spiritual medium that can incorporate a specific spirit guide or Quimbanda spirit to receive spiritual remedies and spiritual solutions to their problems. The spiritual process by which an individual medium becomes possessed by the spirits is referred to as “incorporating the spirit”. The spirits and deities of the Quimbanda religious pantheon are divided into seven categories. These seven categories are known as the ***THE SEVEN GREATER QUIMBANDA KINGDOMS*** and ***THE SEVEN LESSER QUIMBANDA KINGDOMS***. Each one of the Seven Quimbanda Kingdoms is ruled over by a specific set of deities and spirits. Each of the Seven Quimbanda Kingdoms is associated with a specific location, such as the crossroads, cemetery, oceans, forest, mountains and churches. Within the Seven Quimbanda, the first three (3) Kingdoms of Quimbanda deities are more commonly known as the ***QUIMBANDA TRINITY***. The Quimbanda Trinity is composed of the three deities, ***Exu Maioral***, ***Exu Rei*** and ***Maria Padilla Reina***. Together these three powerful spiritual forces govern the cosmos and the Earth for Nzambi. That is why the religious practitioners of the Quimbanda religion venerate these three deities. The veneration of the Quimbanda Trinity is a central spiritual belief of our faith. Religious practitioners of Quimbanda believe that the deities of the Quimbanda pantheon were placed there by Nzambi to watch over the Universe and over the actions of mankind. Within the realm of the outer confines of the Kingdoms of the Quimbanda Trinity there are found the mysteries of the inner Seven Lesser Quimbanda

Kingdoms of the spirit Exu Rei and the spirit Maria Padilla Reina. ***THE SEVEN LESSER QUIMBANDA KINGDOMS*** are collectively ruled over by the deity Exu Rei and the female deity, Maria Padilla Reina. The deity Maria Padilla Reina is also known as Pomba Gira by the religious practitioners of the Quimbanda religious faith. The deity Exu Rei and the deity Maria Padilla Reina are believed to have seven different spiritual paths which are split among ***THE SEVEN LESSER QUIMBANDA KINGDOMS***. Each of ***THE SEVEN LESSER QUIMBANDA KINGDOMS*** is governed over by a distinct spiritual path of the deity Exu Rei and the deity Maria Padilla Reina. Within each of the ***THE SEVEN LESSER QUIMBANDA KINGDOMS***, there are 9 specific Chief Guardian Spirits of Exu and Pombagiras that are associated with a specific spiritual task and assignment to spiritually assist mankind. These Exu and Pombagira spirits operate under the direct command of the King (EXU) and Queen (REINA) that govern a particular Quimbanda Kingdom. Although there are many different individual Exus and Pombagira spirits represented within the confines of ***THE SEVEN LESSER QUIMBANDA KINGDOMS***, it is believed that there exist only 121 different distinct Exus and 121 different distinct Pombagiras. This belief is not shared by all traditional Quimbanda temples and in some temples there could be hundreds.

THE MEANINGS OF THE SEVEN LESSER QUIMBANDA KINGDOMS

The following are the characteristics and spirits associated with each of the ***Seven Lesser Quimbanda Kingdoms of Exu***. In the Quimbanda religion, the Spirit Exu is represented by the masculine spiritual force and the Spirit Pomba Gira is represented by the feminine spiritual force. Together these two spiritual forces are inseparable and represent balance of mind, body, spirit and soul.

The ***First Lesser Quimbanda Kingdom*** of the Spirit Exu is known as ***The Kingdom of the Crossroads*** (*Reino Das Encruzilhadas*). This Kingdom is ruled over and governed by the Spirit, **Exu Rei Das Encruzilhadas** and the Spirit, **Pomba Gira Das Encruzilhadas**. The First Quimbanda Kingdom of the Spirit Exu represents the spiritual energies and forces found at the crossroads. The nine Chief Guardian Exu Spirits found in the First Quimbanda Kingdom are; *Exu Tranca Ruas, Exu Sete Encruzilhadas, Exu Das Almas, Exu Marabo, Exu Tiriri, Exu Veludo, Exu Morcego, Exu Sete Gargalhadas* and *Exu Mirim*.

The ***Second Lesser Quimbanda Kingdom*** of the Spirit Exu is known as ***The Kingdom of the Seven Crossings*** (*Reino Dos Sete Cruzeiros*). This Kingdom is ruled over and governed by the Spirit, **Exu Rei Dos Sete Cruzeiros** and the Spirit, **Pomba Gira Dos Sete Cruzeiros**. The Second Quimbanda Kingdom of the Spirit Exu represents the spiritual energies and forces found at the crossings. The nine Chief Guardian Exu Spirits found in the second Quimbanda Kingdom are; *Exu Tranca Tudo, Exu Kirombo, Exu Sete Cruzeiros, Exu Mangueira, Exu Kaminaloa, Exu Sete Cruzes, Exu 7 Portas, Exu Meia Noite* and *Exu Kalunga*.

The ***Third Lesser Quimbanda Kingdom*** of the Spirit Exu is known as ***The Kingdom of the Forests*** (*Reino Das Matas*). This Kingdom is ruled over and governed by the Spirit, **Exu Rei Das Matas** and the Spirit, **Pomba Gira Das Matas**. The Third Quimbanda Kingdom of the Spirit Exu represents the spiritual energies and forces found within the forests and fields. The nine Chief Guardian Exu Spirits found in the Third Quimbanda Kingdom are; *Exu Quebra Galho, Exu Das Sombras, Exu Das Matas, Exu Das Campinas, Exu Da Serra Negra, Exu Sete Pedras, Exu Sete Cobras, Exu Do Cheiro* and *Exu Arranca Toco*.

The ***Fourth Lesser Quimbanda Kingdom*** of the Spirit Exu is known as ***The Kingdom of the Cemetery*** (*Reino Da Kalunga*). This Kingdom is ruled over and governed by the Spirit, **Exu Rei Kalunga** and the Spirit, **Pomba Gira Kalunga**. The fourth Quimbanda Kingdom of the Spirit Exu represents the spiritual energies and forces found within the mysteries of the cemetery. The nine Chief Guardian Exu Spirits found in the fourth Quimbanda Kingdom are; *Exu Porteira, Exu Sete Tumbas, Exu Sete Catacumbas, Exu Da Brasa, Exu Caveira, Exu Kalunga Pequena, Exu Corcunda, Exu Sete Cova* and *Exu Capa Preta.*

The ***Fifth Lesser Quimbanda Kingdom*** of the Spirit Exu is known as ***The Kingdom of the Souls*** (*Reino Das Almas*). This Kingdom is ruled over and governed by the Spirit, **Exu Rei Das Almas** and the Spirit, **Pomba Gira Das Almas**. The fifth Quimbanda Kingdom of the Spirit Exu represents the spiritual energies and forces found within the mysteries of the world of the dead (afterworld).The nine Chief Guardian Exu Spirits found in the fifth Quimbanda Kingdom are; *Exu Sete Lombas, Exu Pemba, Exu Maraba, Exu Curado, Exu Nove Luzes, Exu 7 Montanhas, Exu Tata Caveira, Exu Gira Mundo* and *Exu 7 Poeiras*.

The ***Sixth Lesser Quimbanda Kingdom*** of the Spirit Exu is known as The Kingdom of the Lyre (Reino Das Liras). This Kingdom is ruled over and governed by the Spirit, **Exu Rei Das Liras** and the Spirit, **Pomba Gira Das Liras**. The fifth Quimbanda Kingdom of the Spirit Exu represents the spiritual energies and forces found within human sexuality, earthly and physical pleasures. The nine Chief Guardian Exu Spirits found in the sixth Quimbanda Kingdom are; *Exu Dos Infernos, Exu Dos Cabares* , *Exu Sete Liras, Exu Cigano, Exu Ze Pelintra, Exu Pagao, Exu Da Ganga, Exu Male* and *Exu Chama Dinheiro*.

The ***Seventh Lesser Quimbanda Kingdom*** of the Spirit Exu is known as The Kingdom of the Beaches (Reino Das 7 Praias). This Kingdom is ruled over and governed by the Spirit, **Exu Rei Das 7 Praias** and the Spirit, **Pomba Gira Das 7 Praias**. The seventh Quimbanda Kingdom of the Spirit Exu represents the spiritual energies and forces found in and around the ocean or bodies of water. The nine Chief Guardian Exu Spirits found in the seventh Quimbanda Kingdom are; *Exu Dos Rios, Exu Das Cachoeiras, Exu Da Pedra Preta, Exu Marinheiro, Exu Do Lodo, Exu Mare, Exu Bahiano, Exu Dos Ventos* and *Exu Do Coco.*

SPELLS & RITUALS OF THE SEVEN LESSER QUIMBANDA KINGDOMS

Knowing the spiritual entities of the Seven Lesser Quimbanda Kingdoms and understanding the meaning of each of them and how they function are key elements in practicing Brazilian Quimbanda, if you want to see fast and successful results in your spells and rituals. The following is a simple explanation of the meaning of the Seven Lesser Quimbanda Kingdoms and how they work.

Spells and rituals of the **First Lesser Quimbanda Kingdom** represent the crossroads of life and everything associated with change. The spiritual requests of the First Lesser Quimbanda Kingdom and or petitions by individuals can be for either good or bad. An example of this would be an individual who has been bewitched or has had a long history of bad luck and misfortune. The spirits of the First Lesser Quimbanda Kingdom can be petitioned to open up the roads to change an individual's luck from bad to good. Typically, spells and rituals of this kingdom are usually done and performed at the crossroads.

Spells and rituals of the **Second Lesser Quimbanda Kingdom** represent the crossings of life and everything associated with the exchange of knowledge and our opinions. The spiritual entities of this kingdom can cause and prevent accidents, bring conflict or calmness between people, can cause ruin and bring tragedy to individuals. The spiritual requests of the Second Lesser Quimbanda Kingdom and or petitions by individuals can be for either good or bad. An example of this would be an individual who has been unjustly accused or spiritually attacked. The spirits of the Second Lesser Quimbanda Kingdom can be petitioned to reverse any and all types of black magic and send it back to an enemy. Typically, spells and rituals of this kingdom are usually done and performed at street crossings.

Spells and rituals of the **Third Lesser Quimbanda Kingdom** represent physical and spiritual growth, healing and all legal matters. The spiritual requests of the Third Lesser Quimbanda Kingdom and or petitions by individuals can be for either good or bad. An example of this would be an individual who is in a legal battle. The spirits of the Third Lesser Quimbanda Kingdom can be petitioned to give the individual a legal victory in a pending lawsuit or legal matter. Typically, spells and rituals of this kingdom are usually done and performed in the forests or mountains.

Spells and rituals of the **Fourth Lesser Quimbanda Kingdom** represent the emotional and spiritual wellbeing of individuals. The spiritual requests of the Fourth Lesser Quimbanda Kingdom and or petitions by individuals can be for either good or bad. An example of this would be an individual who has a constant depression, sickness or who has been bewitched to feel suicidal. The spirits of the Fourth Lesser Quimbanda Kingdom can be petitioned banish away sickness and negative vibrations. Typically, spells and rituals of this kingdom are usually done and performed in the cemetery.

Spells and rituals of the **Fifth Lesser Quimbanda Kingdom** represent the spiritual and physical emotions of the world of the living and the dead. The spiritual requests of the Fifth Lesser Quimbanda Kingdom and or petitions by individuals can be for either good or bad. An example of this would be an individual who has recently lost a loved one in death. The spirits of the Fifth Lesser Quimbanda Kingdom can be petitioned to ensure that their soul crosses over into the spirit world. The spirits of the Fifth Lesser Quimbanda Kingdom can be petitioned to heal an individual of all types of spiritual sickness. Typically, spells and rituals of this kingdom are usually done and performed at high places such as the mountains. Spells and rituals of this kingdom can also be petitioned at hospitals, churches and at funeral parlors.

Spells and rituals of the **Sixth Lesser Quimbanda Kingdom** represent the material and erotic pleasures of life. The spiritual requests of the Sixth Lesser Quimbanda Kingdom and or petitions by individuals can be for either good or bad. An example of this would be an individual who likes to gamble. The spirits of the Sixth Lesser Quimbanda Kingdom can be petitioned to bring success in all games of chance. The spirits of the Sixth Lesser Quimbanda Kingdom can also be petitioned in all matters of lust and seduction. Typically, spells and rituals of this kingdom are usually done and performed at the entrances of banks, casinos, bars and brothels.

Spells and rituals of the **Seventh Lesser Quimbanda Kingdom** represent the emotional moments, spiritual moments and the rise and fall of an individual's life. The spiritual requests of the Seventh Lesser Quimbanda Kingdom and or petitions by individuals can be for either good or bad. An example of this would be an individual who desires marriage. The spirits of the Seventh Lesser Quimbanda Kingdom can be petitioned to bring or to attract a suitable marriage partner. The spirits of the Seventh Quimbanda Kingdom can be petitioned to assist individuals during spiritual purification rituals. Typically, spells and rituals of this kingdom are usually done and performed at the beach or near a body of water.

STEPS TO SUCCESSFUL QUIMBANDA SPELL CASTING

1. *Familiarize yourself with the particular Lesser Quimbanda Kingdom of Exu that you will be working with and all of the Chief Exu Spirits which are guardians of that realm. By familiarizing yourself with the particular Lesser Quimbanda Kingdom you will be able to decide for yourself if you are in the correct place for the particular type of spell that you desire.*

2. *Decide if you will be using the basic spirit signature of the Quimbanda Cross to perform your spell or if you will be using a particular specific spirit signature for the specific type of Exu or Pomba Gira that you will be summoning. If you will be using the general spirit signature of the Quimbanda Cross then you just need to use three colors of candles. These colors are Red, Black and White. If you will be using a specific spirit signature than you will have to decide the appropriate colored candle which will be set directly on top of the spirit signature after you have prepared and dressed the candle.*

3. *Draw or carve the spirit signature of the particular Exu or pomba Gira that you will be summoning and invoking during the ritual directly on the outside of the candle. If you will be using a traditional glass encased religious candle then you can draw the spirit signature with a black permanent ink marker. If you will be carving the spirit signature on a pillar or votive candle, you also have the option to carve your desires of what you want to be the result of the ritual directly on the candle around the spirit signature. You can aalso do the same using the permanent ink marker if you will be using the encased religious glass candle.*

4. *Dress the candle using the appropriate magical occult oils to enhance the power of the magical spell or ritual. Candles can be dressed with one or more different types of occult oils at the same time and rubbed directly onto the candles to achieve better spiritual results.*

5. *Light the appropriate magical occult incense during the ritual to better enhance the magical spell ritual.*

6. *Always use a bell to ring during the magical ritual when invoking the Quimbanda deities to invite them to the ritual. You can design your own prayer for your ritual or you can use the general Quimbanda prayer that I have provided.*

7. *At the end of every ritual, meditate on your desires for 20 to 30 minutes that you perform the ritual.*

8. *Rituals should be done for a series of consecutive days. Normally three consecutive days, seven consecutive days or nine consecutive days, depending on what your desire is and what your spiritual intent is.*

9. *You should always take some kind of ritual spiritual bath before beginning every ritual and you should also cleanse yourself off at the last day of the ritual using African Black Soap or a spiritual bath of your choice.*

10. *Remember, the magic of Quimbanda is very strong and powerful, but you can be creative with your magical spell ritual without having the fear of any negative spiritual consequences.*

A GENERAL RITUAL USING THE QUIMBANDA CROSS

The Quimbanda Cross spirit signature can be used to invoke and summon any of the spirits and deities of the Seven Greater Quimbanda Kingdoms and also for the Seven Lesser Quimbanda Kingdoms.

Draw the Quimbanda Cross using white chalk on the hard surface of a cement floor. You can also draw the spirit signature of the Quimbanda Cross with a permanent black ink marker on a white plate.

After drawing the Quimbanda Cross spirit signature then you will fasten or place a red candle, black candle and a white candle directly into the center of the Quimbanda Cross and light them in that order to begin each magical ritual.

Remember that the candles should be carved with the particular spirit signatures on them and then prepared and dressed with your occult oils before lighting them.

Don't forget to use the appropriate magical occult incense for your desired ritual.

A GENERAL RITUAL TO USE A SPECIFIC EXU SPIRIT SIGNATURE

Draw the spirit signature of the particular Exu or Pomba Gira that you will be spiritually working with.

The spirit signature can be drawn using white chalk on the hard surface of a cement floor. You can also draw the spirit signature of the particular Exu or Pomba Gira with a permanent black ink marker on a white plate.

After drawing the spirit signature then you will fasten or place the ritual invoking candle directly into the center of the spirit signature.

Remember that the candles should be carved with the particular spirit signatures on them and then prepared and dressed with your occult oils before lighting them.

The color of the candle will depend on what type of magical spell or ritual that you will be performing or casting. If you will be hexing someone, then use black. Remember, black candles can be also used for banishing away negative vibrations so please take the time to review the magical color chart before embarking into the world of magical Quimbanda spells and rituals. There are so many color variations that can be used to achieve a desired magical result.

A GENERAL RITUAL PRAYER OF THE SECOND KINGDOM

While lighting the candles recite the following ritual prayers:

IN THE NAME OF NZAMBI, THE GOD OF THE HEAVENS AND THE EARTH - SARAVA

IN THE NAME OF EXU MAIORAL - SARAVA

IN THE NAME OF EXU REI - SARAVA

IN THE NAME OF MARIA PADILLA REINA - SARAVA

IN THE NAME OF THE QUIMBANDA TRINITY - SARAVA

I, say your complete birth name, INVOKE AND DO SUMMON THE DIVINE **KING, EXU REI DOS SETE CRUZEIROS** & **QUEEN, POMBA GIRA REINA DOS SETE CRUZEIROS** OF THE SECOND LESSER QUIMBANDA KINGDOM TO DESCEND UPON THIS SACRED RITUAL AND GIVE IT LIFE.

I, say your complete birth name, INVOKE AND DO SUMMON THE CHIEF GUARDIAN SPIRITS OF THE SECOND QUIMBANDA KINGDOM TO DESCEND UPON THIS SACRED RITUAL AND GIVE IT LIFE.

I ASK YOU O GLORIOUS QUIMBANDA SPIRITS TO PLACE A RING OF LIGHT AROUND ME AND THIS RITUAL AREA SO THAT MY ENEMEIES KNOWN AND UNKNOWN WILL NOT SEE NOR HEAR WHAT IS ABOUT TO BE SAID OR DONE DURING THIS RITUAL.

I DO SUMMON YOUR SPIRIT HERE FROM THE FOUR CORNERS OF THE EARTH AND FROM ABOVE AND FROM BELOW.

O POWERFUL SPIRITS, **KING, EXU REI DOS SETE CRUZEIROS** & **QUEEN, POMBA GIRA REINA DOS SETE CRUZEIROS**, GUARDIAN OF THE SECRETS OF THE CROSSINGS, I KNOCK UPON YOUR SACRED DOOR TO OPEN THE GATES OF THE SEVEN LESSER QUIMBANDA KINGDOMS TO GRANT MY REQUEST- SARAVA

BY THE POWER OF THE SACRED DIVINE NAMES OF THE CHIEF GUARDIAN SPIRITS OF EXU: ***Exu Tranca Tudo***, ***Exu Kirombo***, ***Exu Sete Cruzeiros***, ***Exu Mangueira***, ***Exu Kaminaloa***, ***Exu Sete Cruzes***, ***Exu 7 Portas***, ***Exu Meia Noite***, ***Exu Kalunga***, I DO SUMMON YOU HERE TO GIVE LIGHT IN DARKNESS. - SARAVA

BY THE POWER OF YOUR DIVINE HOLY LEGION OF THE SACRED NINE UNDER YOUR COMMAND, I DO SUMMON: ***Exu Tranca Tudo***, ***Exu Kirombo***, ***Exu Sete Cruzeiros***, ***Exu Mangueira***, ***Exu Kaminaloa***, ***Exu Sete Cruzes***, ***Exu 7 Portas***, ***Exu Meia Noite***, ***Exu Kalunga***, I DO SUMMON YOU HERE TO GIVE LIGHT IN DARKNESS. - SARAVA

O POWERFUL SPIRIT, *say the name of the particular Quimbanda spirit or diety that you are invoking or performing the ritual for,*YOU ARE THE GUARDIAN OF THE MYSTERIES OF THE CROSSINGS AND I AM REQUESTING THAT YOU, *say here what you are spiritually requesting*.

O POWERFUL SPIRIT, *say the name of the particular Quimbanda spirit or diety that you are invoking or performing the ritual for,*AS THE DAY TURNS TO NIGHT AND AS THE NIGHT TURNS TO DAY, SO SHALL MY REQUEST BE GRANTED IN THE NAME OF THE HOLY QUIMBANDA TRINITY. SARAVA

O POWERFUL SPIRITS, ***KING, EXU REI DOS SETE CRUZEIROS*** AND ***QUEEN, POMBA GIRA REINA DOS SETE CRUZEIROS***, IT IS YOU WHO TURNS THE WORLD AT 12 MIDNIGHTAT THE KINGDOM OF THE CROSSINGS - SARAVA

O POWERFUL SPIRITS, ***KING, EXU REI DOS SETE CRUZEIROS*** AND ***QUEEN, POMBA GIRA REINA DOS SETE CRUZEIROS***, IT IS YOU WHO GUARDS THE DOOR TO THE DEAD AT THE KINGDOM OF THE CROSSINGS-SARAVA

O POWERFUL SPIRITS, ***KING, EXU REI DOS SETE CRUZEIROS*** AND ***QUEEN, POMBA GIRA REINA DOS SETE CRUZEIROS***, IT IS YOU WHO LIGHTS THE FIRE OF THE INFERNO AT THE KINGDOM OF THE CROSSINGS-SARAVA

O POWERFUL SPIRITS, ***KING, EXU REI DOS SETE CRUZEIROS*** AND ***QUEEN, POMBA GIRA REINA DOS SETE CRUZEIROS***, IT IS YOU WHO TURNS THE DAY INTO NIGHT AT THE KINGDOM OF THE CROSSINGS-SARAVA

O POWERFUL SPIRITS, ***KING, EXU REI DOS SETE CRUZEIROS*** AND ***QUEEN, POMBA GIRA REINA DOS SETE CRUZEIROS***, IT IS YOU WHO STANDS AT THE DOOR OF THE LIVING AND THE DEAD AT THE KINGDOM OF THE CROSSINGS - SARAVA

O POWERFUL SPIRITS, ***KING, EXU REI DOS SETE CRUZEIROS*** AND ***QUEEN, POMBA GIRA REINA DOS SETE CRUZEIROS***, IT IS YOU WHO HOLDS THE KEY TO THE WORLD OF THE FORBIDDEN MYSTERIES AT THE KINGDOM OF THE CROSSINGS.-SARAVA

O POWERFUL SPIRITS, ***KING, EXU REI DOS SETE CRUZEIROS*** AND ***QUEEN, POMBA GIRA REINA DOS SETE CRUZEIROS***, IT IS YOU WHO WINS THE BATTLE AT 12 MIDNIGHT AT THE CROSSINGS - SARAVA

O POWERFUL SPIRITS, ***KING, EXU REI DOS SETE CRUZEIROS*** AND ***QUEEN, POMBA GIRA REINA DOS SETE CRUZEIROS***, IT IS YOU WHO CONQUERS AND TRIUMPHS OVER OUR ENEMIES - SARAVA.

O POWERFUL SPIRITS, ***KING, EXU REI DOS SETE CRUZEIROS*** AND ***QUEEN, POMBA GIRA REINA DOS SETE CRUZEIROS***, GRANT MY REQUEST ON THIS SACRED NIGHT - SARAVA

O POWERFUL SPIRIT, *say the name of the particular Quimbanda spirit or diety that you are invoking or performing the ritual for,*GRANT MY REQUEST ON THIS SACRED NIGHT - SARAVA

IN THE NAME OF NZAMBI, THE GOD OF THE HEAVENS AND THE EARTH - SARAVA

IN THE NAME OF EXU MAIORAL - SARAVA

IN THE NAME OF EXU REI - SARAVA

IN THE NAME OF MARIA PADILLA REINA - SARAVA

IN THE NAME OF THE QUIMBANDA TRINITY - SARAVA

STATE YOUR REQUEST HERE

THE SECOND LESSER KINGDOM

KINGDOM OF THE CROSSINGS (REINO DOS SETE CRUZEIROS)

Ruling Diety: ***KING, EXU REI DOS SETE CRUZEIROS***

Ruling Diety: ***QUEEN, POMBA GIRA REINA DOS SETE CRUZEIROS***

Exu Tranca Tudo - Chief Guardian Spirit

Exu Kirombo - Chief Guardian Spirit

Exu Sete Cruzeiros - Chief Guardian Spirit

Exu Mangueira - Chief Guardian Spirit

Exu Kaminaloa - Chief Guardian Spirit

Exu Sete Cruzes - Chief Guardian Spirit

Exu 7 Portas - Chief Guardian Spirit

Exu Meia Noite - Chief Guardian Spirit

Exu Kalunga - Chief Guardian Spirit

SACRED ATTRIBUTES OF THE SECOND LESSER QUIMBANDA KINGDOM:

KINGDOM OF THE CROSSINGS (REINO DOS SETE CRUZEIROS)

The colors of the Kingdom of the Crossings are White and Black.

The sacred day of the week of the Kingdom of the Crossings is Saturday.

The planet of the Kingdom of the Crossings is Saturn.

The sacred symbol of the Kingdom of the Crossroads is two tridents crossed forming an X.

The Holy Day of the Year of the Kingdom of the Crossings is January 7.

The sacred numbers of the Kingdom of the Crossings are 7 and 6.

THE MAGICAL SPIRITS OF THE SECOND QUIMBANDA KINGDOM

KING, EXU REI DOS SETE CRUZEIROS

Kingdom of the Crossings (Reino Dos Sete Cruzeiros). Used to invoke the male energies of the Second Lesser Quimbanda Kingdom for spells and rituals of spiritual growth, healing, legal matters and to open your roads.

QUEEN, POMBA GIRA REINA DOS SETE CRUZEIROS

Kingdom of the Crossings (Reino Dos Sete Cruzeiros).Used to invoke the female energies of the Second Lesser Quimbanda Kingdom for spells and rituals of spiritual growth, healing and legal matters and to open your roads.

EXU TRANCA TUDO

Kingdom of the Crossings (Reino Dos Sete Cruzeiros). Used in spells and rituals to lock up everybody, everything and to turn your enemies luck into bad luck.

EXU KIROMBO

Kingdom of the Crossings (Reino Dos Sete Cruzeiros). Used in spells and rituals to bring abundance of wealth and material wealth to an individual.

EXU SETE CRUZEIROS

Kingdom of the Crossings (Reino Dos Sete Cruzeiros). Used in spells and rituals to astral travel safely.

EXU MANGUEIRA

Kingdom of the Crossings (Reino Dos Sete Cruzeiros). Used in spells and rituals to bewitch an individual for lust, desire, romance and love.

EXU KAMINALOA

Kingdom of the Crossings (Reino Dos Sete Cruzeiros). Used in spells and rituals to attract a mate or to influence a desired individual for love, romance and passion.

EXU SETE CRUZES

Kingdom of the Crossings (Reino Dos Sete Cruzeiros). Used in spells and rituals to find out what your enemies are doing.

EXU 7 PORTAS

Kingdom of the Crossings (Reino Dos Sete Cruzeiros). Used in spells and rituals to open up the door to opportunities that were previously unavailable to you before.

EXU MEIA NOITE

Kingdom of the Crossings (Reino Dos Sete Cruzeiros). Used in spells and rituals to invoke the powers of the dead. Used to give an individual the power over the spoken word to convince and dominate people.

EXU KALUNGA PEQUENA

Kingdom of the Crossings (Reino Dos Sete Cruzeiros). Used in spells and rituals to give an individual supernatural power and command over the spirit world. Also use to dominate and control an individual for love and romance.

A LIST OF CANDLE COLORS AND THEIR MAGICAL MEANINGS

Candles can be fix/dressed with occult oils and burned in magical invocations to seek love, wealth, health, fortune, exorcise evil and cast spells. If you want to see good results with your magical spells then use the following candle color combinations and following their magical meanings. All of the following candle color combinations can be used with any of the Exu Spirits and the Pomba Gira Spirits depending upon the desired magical intent of your spell. If you are unable to find these magical colored combination candles then you can use the following general colors for your spiritual work. A red candle is used to generally represent the Quimbanda Spirit, Exu Maioral, a black candle is generally used to represent the Quimbanda Spirit, Exu Rei and a White candle is generally used to represent the Quimbanda Spirit, Pomba Gira.

BLACK

Used in hexing and cursing spells and rituals. Black candles can also be used to unhex and to banish away negativity.

RED

Passion, energy, power, strength, courage, achievement, magnetism, counteract fatigue and anger.

ORANGE

Attraction, motivation, mental energy, clear thinking, harmony, expansion, happiness.

WHITE

Protection, meditation, blessing, purity, health, and spiritual growth.

GRAY

Neutralizing, stops stress, masking, veiling, and hesitation.

LAVENDER

Spiritual development, psychic growth, divination, blessings, sensitivity.

PINK

Emotional love, romances, and new loves, come to me, friendship.

GOLD

Solar energy, power, physical strength, success, achievement, mental growth.

WHITE & GREEN

Protection of money, i.e. protecting one's investment.

WHITE & PINK

Protecting the harmony and love of a relationship.

WHITE & BLACK

Jinx removing, removing nasty vibes.

WHITE & PURPLE

Excellent meditation candle.

WHITE & BLUE

Protection and peace in home.

WHITE & YELLOW

Cleansing of your aura.

WHITE & ORANGE

Blessing and harmony in the home.

WHITE & RED

Protects your health.

WHITE & BROWN

Protection of children and your pets.

GREEN & BROWN

Attracting good job, proper home.

GREEN & BLUE

Prosperity.

GREEN & PURPLE

Attracting large amounts of money.

GREEN & BLACK

Banishing poverty or money problems.

RED & BROWN

Favor in legal matters.

RED & BLACK

Reversing negativity or evil to sender.

RED & PURPLE

Conquering difficult situations.

RED & GREEN

Powerful money boost for raises and promotions.

BLUE & PURPLE

Prophetic dreams.

BLUE & BLACK

Removing depression.

YELLOW & RED

Attracting love.

YELLOW & GREEN

Attracting success and money.

YELLOW & BLUE

Achieving balance.

YELLOW & BROWN

Renting or selling of a home, success.

YELLOW & BLACK

Banishing bad luck, removing blocks in your success.

YELLOW & PURPLE

Promotions, new endeavors.

YELLOW & ORANGE

Attracting success, fast luck.

ORANGE & RED

Attracting a perfect mate, solar energy.

ORANGE & YELLOW

Attracting success in the arts, music.

ORANGE & GREEN

Balance and expansion, fast luck.

ORANGE & PURPLE

Aids in studying, also power and strength.

ORANGE & BROWN

Attracts harmony, business success.

ORANGE & BLUE

Happiness, harmony, peace and clarity.

ORANGE & BLACK

Removing blocks in business success.

PINK & GREEN

Attracting a mate with money.

PINK & RED

Romance and lust in a relationship.

PINK & PURPLE

For "Come To Me Spells."

PINK & BLUE

Peace and harmony.

PINK & BROWN

Happiness and stability.

WHITE/RED/BROWN

When bad thing happen to good people.When you are not at fault, court, custody, licensing, IRS, etc.

WHITE/RED/PURPLE

When you are at fault, when you need help in overcoming a situation.

WHITE/RED/GREEN

When creditors are a bother, when wishing to attract wages to re-assess how to financially pro-ceed without interference.

WHITE/RED/BLUE

Protect my home and/or my love from all interference.

WHITE/RED/BLACK

For troubles such as magnitude, you need to dispose of quickly, so your thoughts are clear. To divine a solution burn in waning moon for protection against interference.

WHITE/LAVANDER/BLUE

Any time you have truly lost direction, when all you have worked for has gone astray because of loss of faith in yourself and your higher power re-establishes your faith.

WHITE/GRAY/BLACK

For court cases when you are guilty, no evidence against you will be found, charges will be dropped. A sacrifice goes with this; make your sacrifice before hand, whether it is your time, physical or monetary to those who need help.

YELLOW/GREEN/BROWN

For perfect job, attract it, get the money you want and now keep it.

YELLOW/GREEN/PURPLE

When asking for job promotion or raise, also used to increase your $$$. Note: Must have some $$$ first to do this.

YELLOW/PINK/RED

Communication with someone who's friendly to you but you would like more, a stronger bond of interaction.

YELLOW/ORANGE/RED

To attract to you the most important mate that you can have this lifetime. It is essential that you specify all situations that will be compatible with your needs.

PINK/LAVANDER/RED

When your love life has reached an impasse. To re-establish the romance and communication between both of you and the passion that may have been forgotten.

PINK/RED/PURPLE

Re-establish by attracting them back with thoughts of lust and sexual desire. Also brings someone to you with the intent of deeper passion and a sexual relationship.

PINK/BLUE/BROWN

Burn when it is necessary to have peace, Love and Harmony in the home, especially when adult children are involved.

ORANGE/RED/PURPLE

Mandatory when breaking through those difficult situations.Especially those that involve special favor with authorities, maybe government agencies or legal problems.

THE QUIMBANDA SPIRIT SIGNATURES (PONTOS RISCADOS)

In the Quimbanda magico-religious tradition, spirit signature sigils (a sacred mystical seal) are symbols connected to a set of ideas by which spirits or deities may be summoned to awareness and controlled. The spirit signature sigils connect the spirits to our earthly realm. In the Portuguese language they are called *"Pontos Riscados"*. The spirit signature sigils when used in the appropriate magical manner open up the doors to world of the supernatural. They are used in divinatory practices. The spirit signature sigil itself when drawn out on the ground or drawn on an object will call forth the spirit. The spirit signature sigil also serves as a physical focus through which the Quimbanda Priest achieves the desired state of mind. Spirit signature sigils represent the secret names of spirits and deities who manifest themselves differently to each magic practitioner. Once the Quimbanda Priest has summoned the spirit or deity he may control it, if necessary, by subjecting its sigil to fire or the use of a magical sword or machete. Spirit signature sigils can also serve as amulets, talismans, or meditation tools. Quimbanda spirit signature sigils may be of various signs, such as crosses, tridents, stars associated with different deities. Quimbanda Priests often times inscribe the spirit signature sigil on ceremonial ritual objects, candles or objects of silver, brass, gold, or glass. Such spirit signatures sigils are considered to be magically powerful. Quimbanda Priests also draw these very sacred and powerful spirit signature sigils directly on the ground in front of the spirit ngangas of the Quimbanda Spirits to invoke and to summon the deities to appear and to send them to do their bidding. The following Quimbanda spirit signature sigils (Pontos Riscados) can be used when doing the Quimbanda magical spells and rituals from this book and when making magical talismans and amulets.

A DIAGRAM SHOWING THE SACRED SPIRIT SIGNATURE OF THE QUIMBANDA CROSS.

This Spirit Signature represents the Kingdom of the Crossings and the collective masculine energy of Exu Rei Dos Sete Cruzeiros and the feminine energy of Pomba Gira Reina Dos Sete Cruzeiros together.

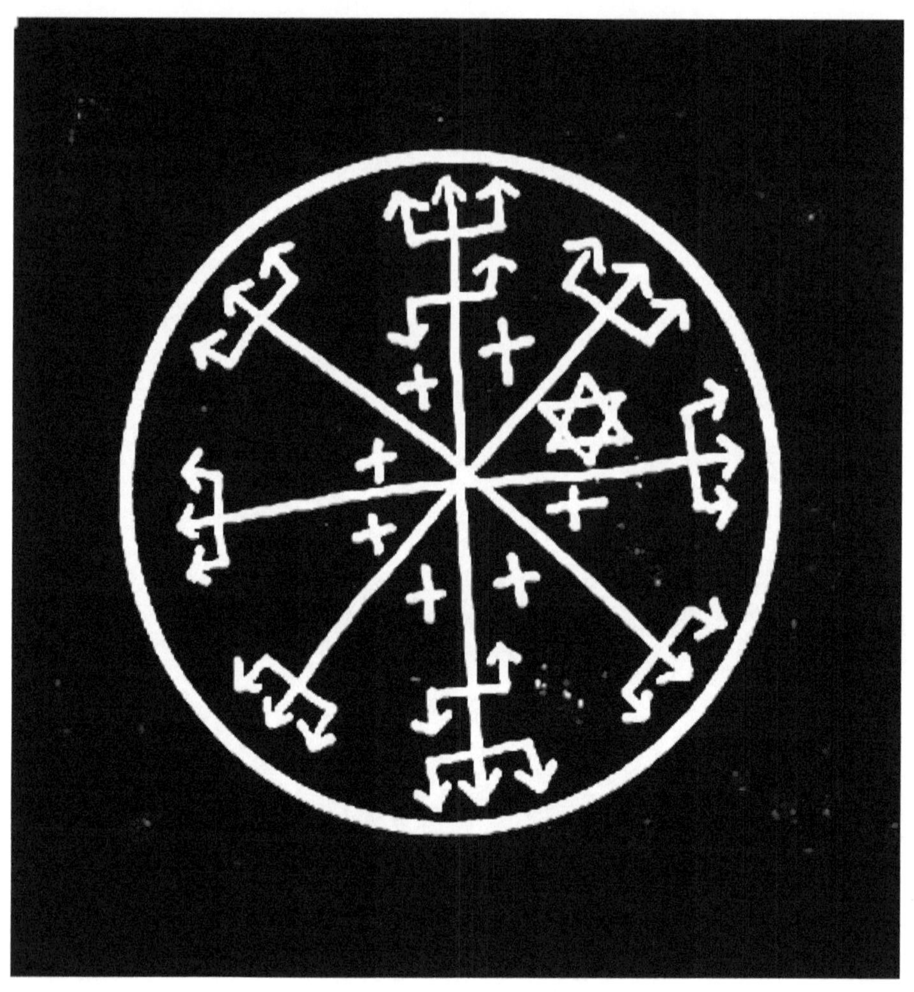

KING, EXU REI DOS SETE CRUZEIROS

Kingdom of the Crossings (Reino Dos Sete Cruzeiros). Used to invoke the male energies of the Second Lesser Quimbanda Kingdom for spells and rituals of spiritual growth, healing, legal matters and to open your roads.

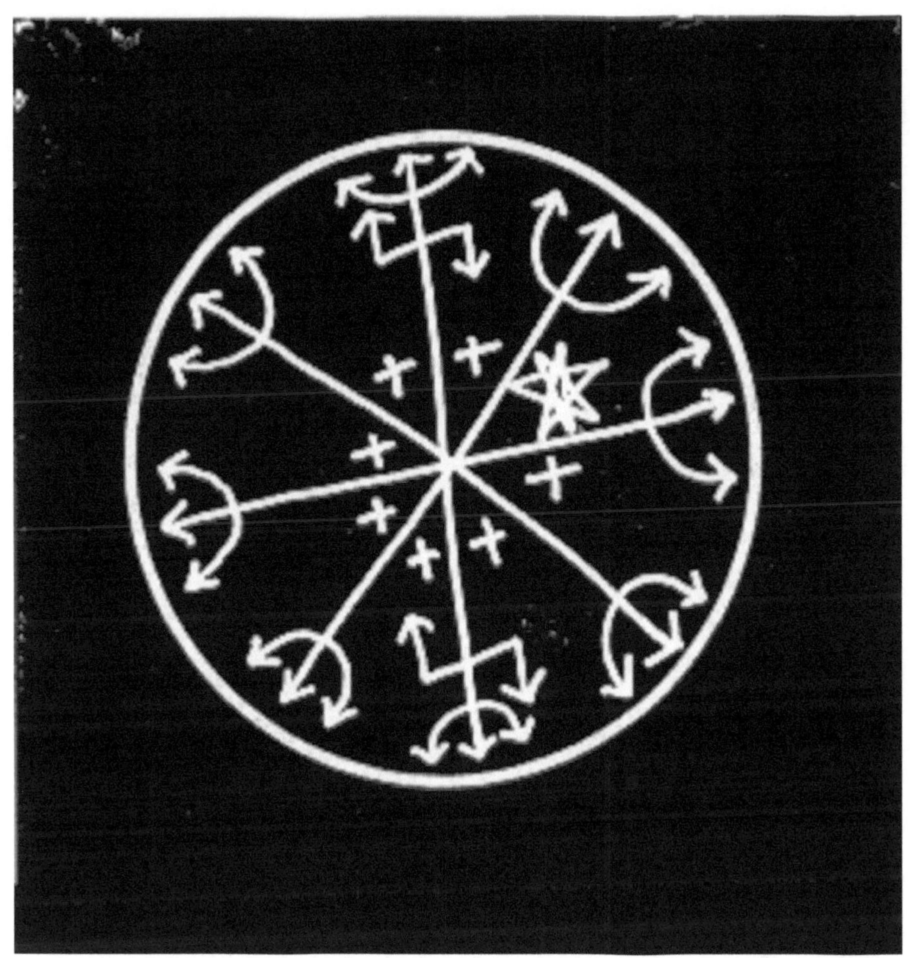

QUEEN, POMBA GIRA REINA DOS SETE CRUZEIROS

Kingdom of the Crossings (Reino Dos Sete Cruzeiros).Used to invoke the female energies of the Second Lesser Quimbanda Kingdom for spells and rituals of spiritual growth, healing and legal matters and to open your roads.

EXU TRANCA TUDO

Kingdom of the Crossings (Reino Dos Sete Cruzeiros). Used in spells and rituals to lock up everybody, everything and to turn your enemies luck into bad luck.

EXU KIROMBO

Kingdom of the Crossings (Reino Dos Sete Cruzeiros). Used in spells and rituals to bring abundance of wealth and material wealth to an individual.

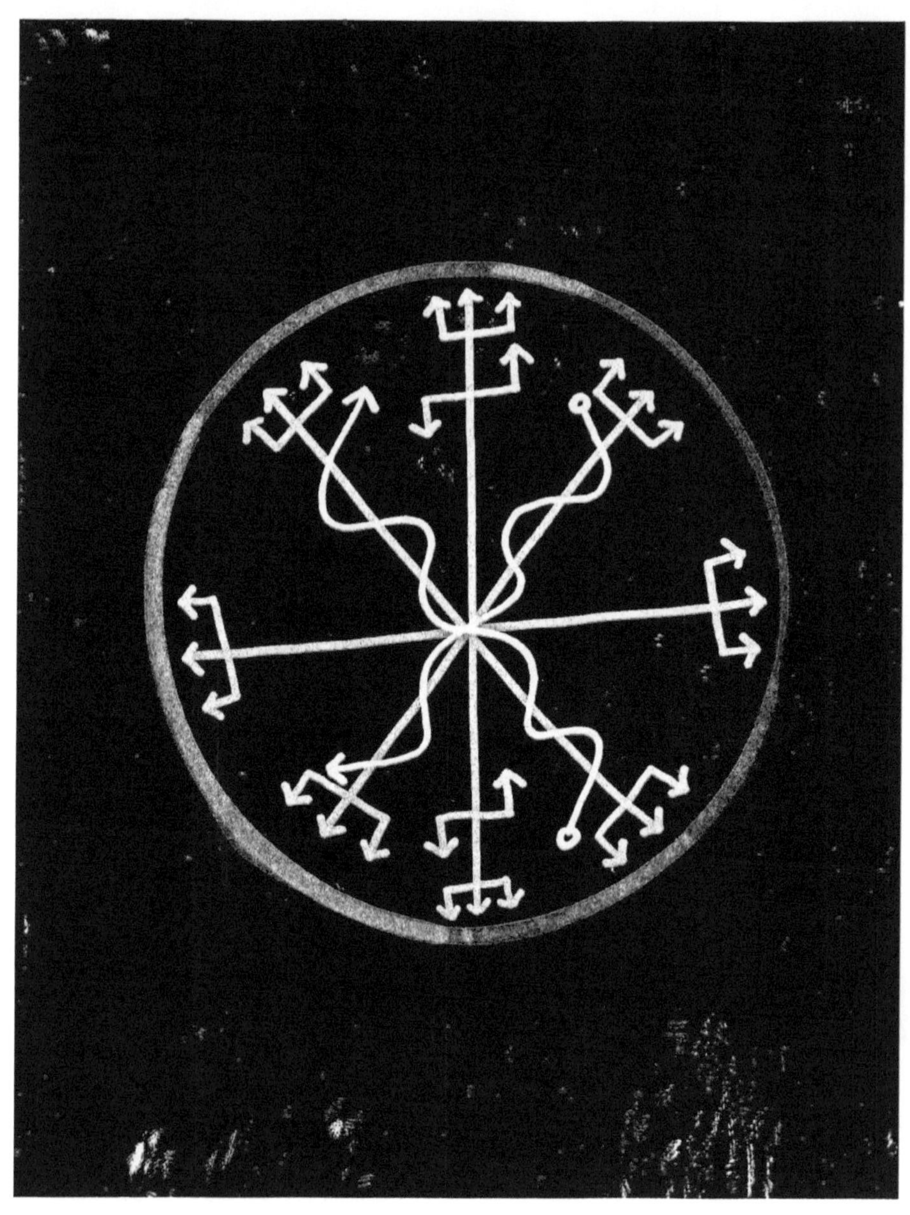

EXU SETE CRUZEIROS

Kingdom of the Crossings (Reino Dos Sete Cruzeiros). Used in spells and rituals to astral travel safely.

EXU MANGUEIRA

Kingdom of the Crossings (Reino Dos Sete Cruzeiros). Used in spells and rituals to bewitch an individual for lust, desire, romance and love.

EXU KAMINALOA

Kingdom of the Crossings (Reino Dos Sete Cruzeiros). Used in spells and rituals to attract a mate or to influence a desired individual for love, romance and passion.

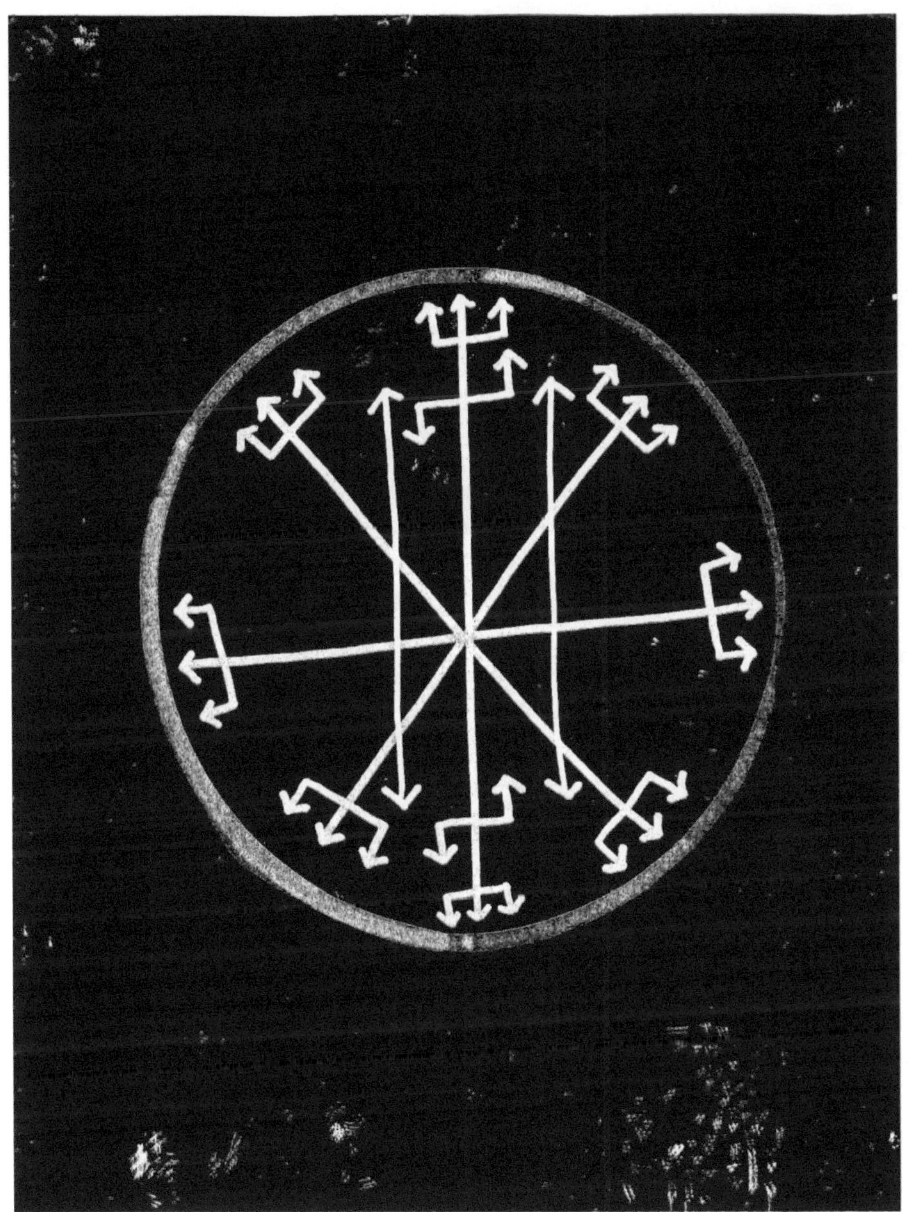

EXU SETE CRUZES

Kingdom of the Crossings (Reino Dos Sete Cruzeiros). Used in spells and rituals to find out what your enemies are doing.

EXU 7 PORTAS

Kingdom of the Crossings (Reino Dos Sete Cruzeiros). Used in spells and rituals to open up the door to opportunities that were previously unavailable to you before.

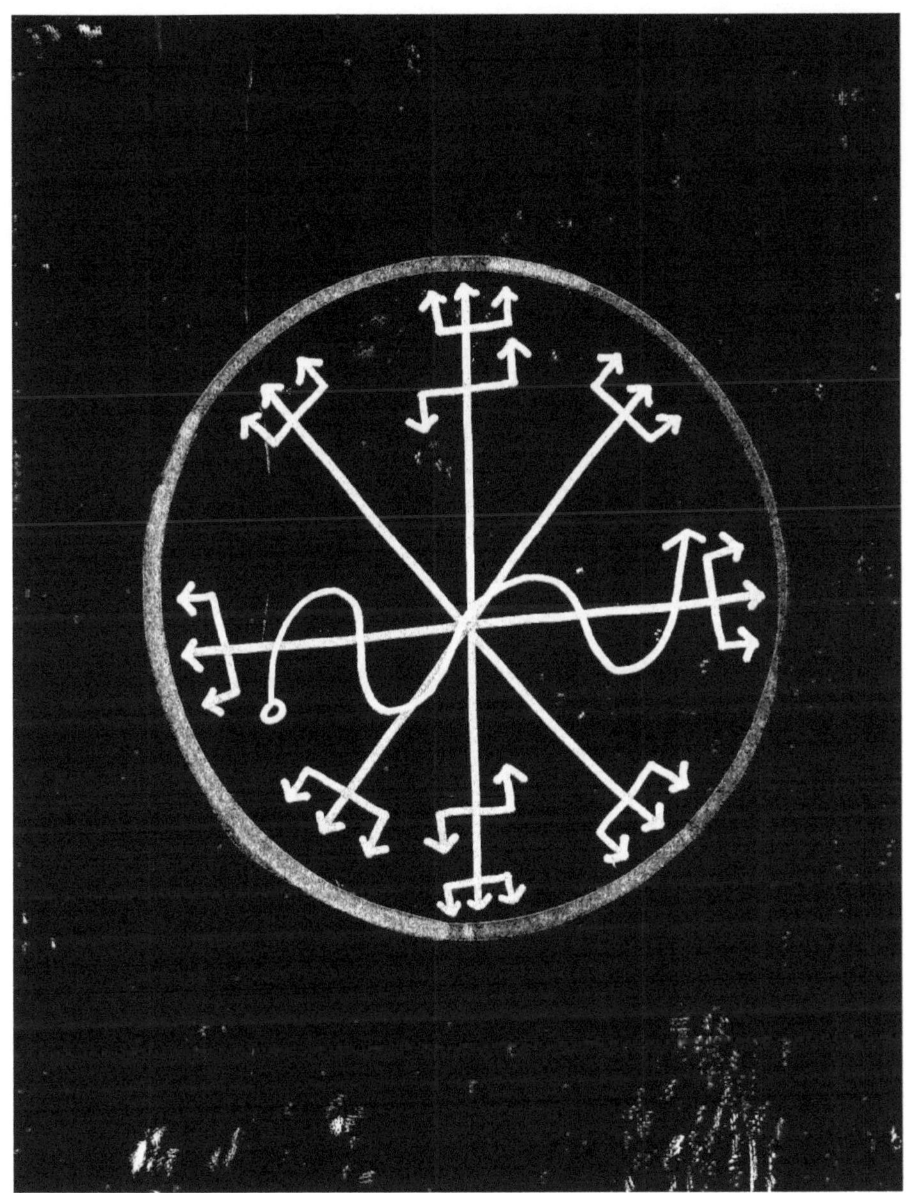

EXU MEIA NOITE

Kingdom of the Crossings (Reino Dos Sete Cruzeiros). Used in spells and rituals to invoke the powers of the dead. Used to give an individual the power over the spoken word to convince and dominate people.

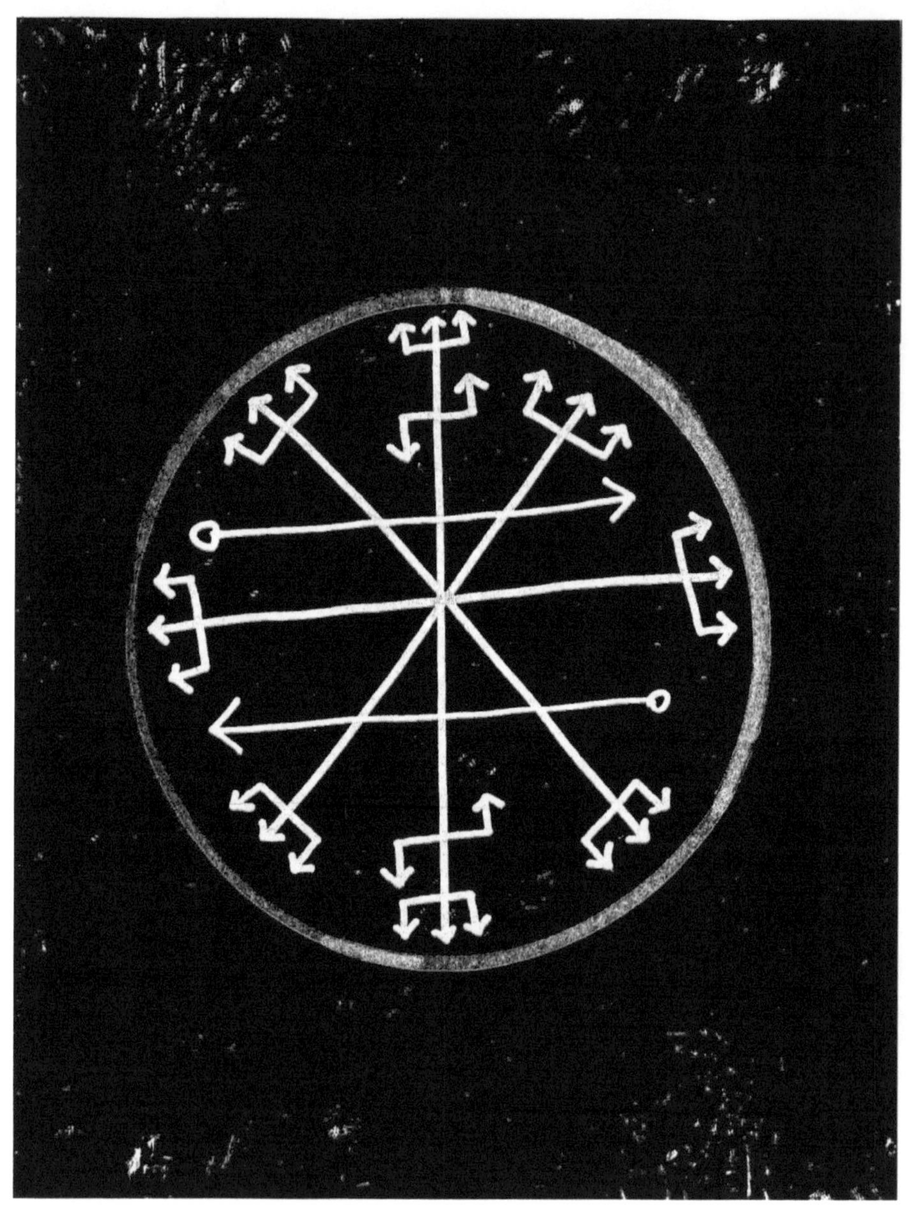

EXU KALUNGA PEQUENA

Kingdom of the Crossings (Reino Dos Sete Cruzeiros). Used in spells and rituals to give an individual supernatural power and command over the spirit world. Also use to dominate and control an individual for love and romance.

SPIRITUAL OIL
SPIRITUAL OIL
SPIRITUAL OIL
SPIRITUAL OIL

www.ingramcontent.com/pod-product-compliance
Ingram Content Group UK Ltd.
Pitfield, Milton Keynes, MK11 3LW, UK
UKHW041923190726
13854UKWH00003B/1409

9 781105 751103